INTO THE UNKNOWN

CRYPTIDS AND CREATURES

Kevin Cunningham

Mitchell Lane
PUBLISHERS

Mitchell Lane
PUBLISHERS

mitchelllanepub.com

2001 SW 31st Avenue
Hallandale, FL 33009

First Edition, 2026.
Author: Kevin Cunningham
Designer: Ed Morgan
Editor: Morgan Brody

Series: Into the Unknown
Title: Cryptids and Creatures

Library bound ISBN: 979-8-89260-734-6
eBook ISBN: 979-8-89260-745-2

Photo credits: cover, p. 11, 13, 19, 23, 25 Shutterstock; p. 2, 3, 4, 21, 32 freepik.com; p. 6, 7, 9 wikimedia; p. 17 loc.getarchive.net; catalog.archives.gov

CONTENTS

CHAPTER ONE

WILD MAN OF THE SNOWS

C. K. Howard-Bury led British mountain climbers in 1921. The team explored Mount Everest. Sherpa people belonged to the party. Sherpas live in the Himalayan Mountains. Some work guiding and carrying equipment for climbers.

The team reached a mountain pass. Climbers saw movement above them. They watched with binoculars. Ape-like creatures walked over an open area on two legs.

Some of the Sherpas found giant footprints. Howard-Bury described the prints as "three times those of normal humans." The Sherpas told him a story. A wild man of the snows lived high up the mountains.

CHAPTER ONE

Henry Newman reported for a newspaper. He listened to the expedition's wild man stories. But Newman or Howard-Bury made a mistake. One or both misunderstood the Sherpa language. Newman heard filthy man instead of wild man. He wrote an article. It stated the Howard-Bury team saw the **Abominable** Snowman.

Later, the public began to use the word Yeti. Yeti meant something like "rock-bear" in the Tibetan language. People in mountain communities told **folktales**. Yeti-like creatures had appeared in these stories for 6,000 years in places like Nepal, Bhutan, and Tibet.

The Yeti is one of the most famous cryptids. The word *cryptid* describes mysterious animals that no one can prove exist. Swamp, forest, mountains, lakes, even towns—people around the world report cryptids in many places.

FAST FACT

The Sherpa people live in the eastern Himalayan Mountains. Their bodies can handle the thin air found at high altitudes. Many Sherpas raise yaks and grow potatoes.

CHAPTER TWO

WORLD OF MONSTERS

A cryptid frightened two couples in 1966. Roger Scarberry drove near Pleasant Point, West Virginia. A shape up to 7 feet (2.1 meters) tall appeared. It had red eyes. It had wings. Scarberry sped off.

Local people named the creature Mothman.

CHAPTER TWO

Flying cryptids appear in many places. A glowing reptile named the Ropen glides over New Guinea. The Jersey Devil appears around a New Jersey forest.

The Yeti isn't the only **humanoid** cryptid. Folktales say the Lougarou lurks in Haiti. Australians talk about the Yowie and similar giant creatures. The Chuchunya pops up in Russia.

Thousands in the United Kingdom have seen phantom cats. The shapes look like panthers or mountain lions. Hunters and others report big cats in New Zealand.

FAST FACT

A cryptid may become part of a community. Mothman is a symbol of Point Pleasant. The town raised a metal Mothman statue. Thousands attend a Mothman festival in September. A Mothman museum opened in 2006. A book and film made people more curious about the story.

CHAPTER TWO

Totally unknown creatures startle people, too. The Chupacabra first appeared in Puerto Rico in the 1980s. Today the cryptid turns up across Latin America. The Nandi people of Kenya spoke of a fierce bear-hyena. English-speakers nicknamed it the Nandi bear.

Cryptids also include animals considered extinct. Adventurers search for Mokele-mbembe in the Republic of Congo. Some wonder if the lake monster is a species of dinosaur. The Tasmanian tiger became extinct in the 1930s. But people in Indonesia have described a similar animal.

FAST FACT

People find living animals considered extinct. In 1938, a South African fishing boat brought up a coelacanth. The boat captain called museum official Marjorie Courtenay-Latimer to report the odd fish. She saved the fish's body. The world soon learned the coelacanth had not gone extinct 66 million years ago.

CHAPTER THREE

THEY WANT TO BELIEVE

Cryptozoologists study cryptids. A cryptozoologist gets information from folktales and stories. Scientists prefer evidence like bones.

Eric Shipton photographed huge prints in the Himalayas. His image became famous evidence of the Yeti. A Sherpa man named Sen Tensing told the expedition two kinds of Yeti existed.

CHAPTER THREE

Don Whillans saw Yeti tracks during a 1970 mountain climbing trip. He said he spotted the creature.

"All of a sudden it went right across the hillside for half a mile," he told Reuters. "Its movements seemed ape-like, moving on all fours and going sideways just like a monkey."

Jeffrey McNeely and Edward W. Cronin worked as scientists. Their scientific mission found a line of tracks in Nepal. The pair thought the tracks belonged to a **biped**. Their photos seemed like more strong evidence.

FAST FACT

Ivan T. Sanderson was one of the first cryptozoologists. He first studied real science. Sanderson had a long history with animals and cryptids. He claimed a cryptid bat attacked him in Africa. In 1961, he wrote a book on the Abominable Snowman. Sanderson also kept rare animals in his apartment in New York City.

CHAPTER THREE

People have also claimed to find Yeti body parts. The **relics** included hair, bones, and skin.

Tibetan monks kept the bones of a Yeti hand. The monks raised money showing the hand to visitors. A finger disappeared in the 1950s. Visitors smuggled it to the United Kingdom. A museum misplaced it. Later the staff found the finger bone. It became a part of Yeti history.

FAST FACT

Jeffrey McNeely and Edward W. Cronin looked for the Yeti in the Barun Valley. Humans no longer live in the valley. It is inside one of Nepal's national parks. Mount Makalu, the world's fifth-tallest mountain, towers nearby.

CHAPTER FOUR

INVESTIGATIONS

A **skeptic** hears a cryptid story. They answer: "Show me the evidence."

Footprints and relics convinced some people the Yeti existed. Others thought a Yeti seemed possible.

A skeptic doubts or questions an idea. Yeti skeptics disbelieved the evidence.

Michael Ward explored with Eric Shipton. Ward doubted the Yeti existed. People high in the mountains walked barefoot at times, he noted. A human or animal footprint in melting snow may expand to a giant size.

Lawrence Swan agreed. Giant tracks shocked the biologist. He followed the trail. The tracks got smaller. At the end he saw a fox had made the prints. Wind and melting snow had made some of them bigger.

CHAPTER FOUR

Daniel Taylor worked with people living in the Himalayas. In 1983, he took the footprint of a zoo's Asian black bear. It matched all the prints Shipton photographed.

Yeti body parts failed to pass the evidence test.

Scientist Charlotte Lindqvist tested nine Yeti relics. The monks' Yeti hand belonged to a black bear. In all, eight of the relics came from bears. The ninth was a dog tooth.

"We didn't set out to **debunk** the myth," Lindqvist told CNN.com in 2017. "Clearly, a big part of the Yeti legend has to do with bears," she said at the University of Buffalo.

Adventurers climb the Himalayas to search for the Yeti. New sightings make the news. But often the stories concern fakes and tricks.

FAST FACT

In 2020, Nepal's government used a friendly looking Yeti mascot to attract tourists. But Nepalis complained about the chubby Yeti's appearance. "It looks like a wrestler, not a yeti," Krishna Lama told BBC.com.

CHAPTER FIVE

MAKING UP STORIES

A person plays a **hoax**. Why? Many reasons. The hoaxer may want attention. They hope to make money in some way. They want to add to the cryptid folktales.

Russian scientists met in 2011. The team said it found evidence of a Yeti. An investigator had taken hairs from a Yeti's cave. He sent the hairs to be tested.

Skeptics asked a question. Why did the team take no pictures of the cave? One newspaper offered a **motive** for the Yeti story. It said the local government hoped to drum up **cryptid tourism**.

CHAPTER FIVE

The newspaper guessed it right. A former government official admitted to the hoax in 2021. The fake Yeti lived in a remote area. The government hoped Yeti seekers would visit and spend money.

Travelers seek cryptids far away. They search for the Yeti in Bhutan or Nepal. Cryptid tourism draws thousands of tourists to new places.

Why does cryptid tourism make money? Why do people travel thousands of miles to seek animals that may not exist?

"People have always been fascinated by things in nature which confuse us, things which we just don't understand," cryptozoologist Gary Opit told Nationalgeographic.com.

Skeptics say Charlotte Lindqvist's research solved the Yeti mystery. But people who believe in cryptids keep looking for the creature.

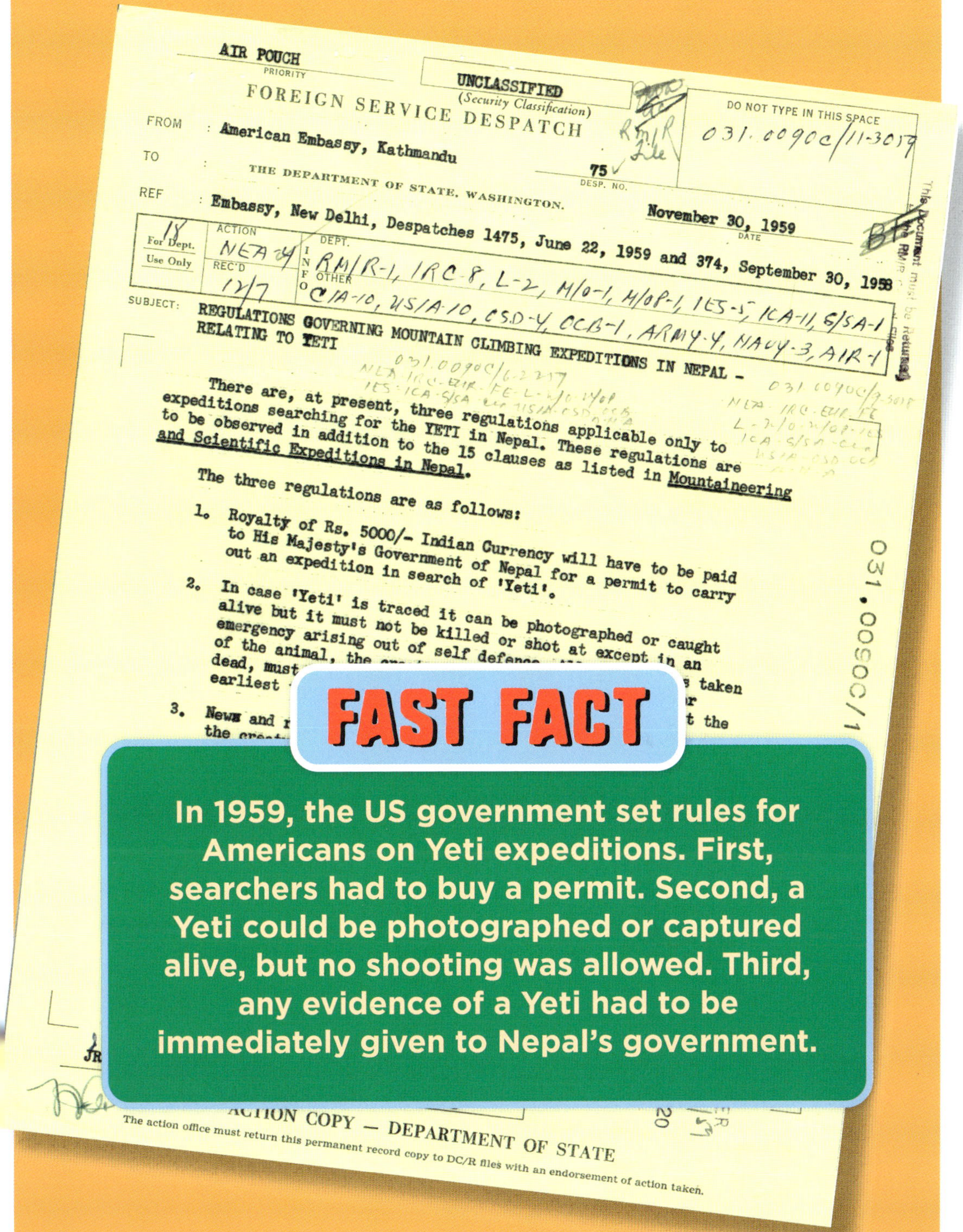

AIR POUCH
PRIORITY

UNCLASSIFIED
(Security Classification)

FOREIGN SERVICE DESPATCH

DO NOT TYPE IN THIS SPACE
031.0090c/11-3059

FROM : American Embassy, Kathmandu

TO : THE DEPARTMENT OF STATE, WASHINGTON.

75
DESP. NO.

REF : Embassy, New Delhi, Despatches 1475, June 22, 1959 and 374, September 30, 1958

November 30, 1959
DATE

For Dept. Use Only — ACTION NEA-4 — REC'D 12/7 — DEPT. RM/R-1, IRC-8, L-2, M/0-1, M/OP-1, IES-5, ICA-11, S/SA-1 — OTHER CIA-10, USIA-10, CSD-4, OCB-1, ARMY-4, NAVY-3, AIR-1

SUBJECT: REGULATIONS GOVERNING MOUNTAIN CLIMBING EXPEDITIONS IN NEPAL - RELATING TO YETI

There are, at present, three regulations applicable only to expeditions searching for the YETI in Nepal. These regulations are to be observed in addition to the 15 clauses as listed in Mountaineering and Scientific Expeditions in Nepal.

The three regulations are as follows:

1. Royalty of Rs. 5000/- Indian Currency will have to be paid to His Majesty's Government of Nepal for a permit to carry out an expedition in search of 'Yeti'.

2. In case 'Yeti' is traced it can be photographed or caught alive but it must not be killed or shot at except in an emergency arising out of self defence ... of the animal, the ... dead, must ... earliest ...

3. News and r... the creat...

ACTION COPY — DEPARTMENT OF STATE

The action office must return this permanent record copy to DC/R files with an endorsement of action taken.

FAST FACT

In 1959, the US government set rules for Americans on Yeti expeditions. First, searchers had to buy a permit. Second, a Yeti could be photographed or captured alive, but no shooting was allowed. Third, any evidence of a Yeti had to be immediately given to Nepal's government.

TIMELINE

4,000 BCE	Himalayan peoples tell stories of hairy giants in the mountains
1921	Sherpa guides tell Charles Howard-Bury about a wild man of the snows
1951	Eric Shipton and Michael Ward photograph huge footprints in the Himalayas
1966	Mothman makes its first appearance near Pleasant Point, West Virginia
1970	Don Whillans claims to see a Yeti while mountain climbing
1980s	The Chupacabra first appears in Puerto Rico
2011	Russian scientists claim they have found a Yeti cave
2017	A team led by Charlotte Lindqvist announces Yeti relics mostly come from bears
2021	A Russian official admits the Yeti cave story was a hoax

GLOSSARY

abominable (a-BOM-eh-na-bul)
Very bad or unpleasant

biped (BY-ped)
An animal that uses two legs to walk

cryptid tourism (KRIP-tid TOOR-iz-em)
A type of travel that uses a local cryptid to draw people to the area

cryptozoologist (KRIP-tow-zoo-AH-le-jist)
A person who studies and searches for animals that may or may not exist

debunk (DEE-bunk)
Disprove a false claim

folktales (FOK-tayl)
Stories shared by a group or community of people

hoax (HOKS)
A fake or trick used to deceive others

humanoid (HYU-me-noyd)
A nonhuman creature with traits that resemble those of a human

motive (MO-tiv)
The reason for doing something

relic (REH-lik)
An object considered valuable because it is associated with a famous figure

skeptic (SKEP-tik)
A person who doubts or questions an idea

FACT CHECK

1. **Yeti sightings take place in which mountain range?**

   A. Andes
   B. Himalayas
   C. Atlas
   D. Rockies

2. **Some Sherpa people describe the Yeti with words that roughly mean which phrase?**

   A. Wild man of the snows
   B. Jersey Devil
   C. The watcher in the water
   D. The king of Mount Everest

3. **Which of the following are considered cryptids?**

   A. Mothman
   B. Chupacabra
   C. Bigfoot
   D. All of the above

4. **Tests on Yeti relics showed most of the objects came from which animal?**

   A. Bears
   B. Snow leopards
   C. Yaks
   D. Apes

Answers: B, A, D, A

FIND OUT MORE

IN PRINT

Anderhagen, Anna. *Chasing the Chupacabra*. Edina, MN: Abdo Group, 2023.

Harper, Ben. T*he Secret Life of the Yeti*. North Mankato, MN: Capstone, 2023.

Hubbard, Ben. *What Do We Know about the Yeti?* New York: Penguin Workshop, 2024.

ON THE INTERNET

Animal Planet. "Nepali Monks Have Kept an Alleged Yeti Hand for Decades." Animal Planet via YouTube. Online Video.
www.youtube.com/watch?v=0Y6Z0YRTz6o

National Geographic. "Evidence of the Yeti." National Geographic via YouTube. Online video.
www.youtube.com/watch?v=LZnAo_2cpYY

Public Broadcasting Service. "The Crazed Hunt for the Himalayan Yeti." Monstrum via PBS.org
www.pbs.org/video/the-crazed-hunt-for-the-himalayan-yeti-f396zr

INDEX

About the Author

Kevin Cunningham has written over 120 books on history, medicine, careers, and climate change. He lives near Chicago, Illinois. Though he finds it hard to believe in the Yeti, he likes cryptid stories.